ANIMAL SNACKERS

DODD, MEAD & COMPANY · NEW YORK

ANIMAL SNACKERS

BETSY LEWIN

Photography by Vincent Colabella; jacket photography by Robert Osonitsch

1 2 3 4 5 6 7 8 9 10

Library of Congress Cataloging in Publication Data

Lewin, Betsy.
    Animal snackers.

    SUMMARY: Brief rhymes describe the favorite food
of various animals. Includes recipe for making bread-
dough animals.
    1. Animals—Juvenile poetry. [1. Animals—Food
habits—Poetry. 2. American poetry] I. Title.
PS3562.E9279A83   811'.5'4   79-24483
ISBN 0-396-07782-X

For Jerky—
    who was the greatest animal snacker of them all

JUST IMAGINE

Imagine if we all could eat
nothing but our favorite treat,

Abandoning with glee sublime
breakfast, lunch, and dinnertime,

Eating where and when we're able,
never seated at a table.

ORILLA

Gorillas, though they look like brutes,
may snack on tender bamboo shoots.

The sight of them may shiver us,
but they are not carnivorous.

PLATYPUS

The platypus is odd enough
with fur and ducklike bill.

He thinks worms are delicious stuff,
which makes him odder still.

OSTRICH

The ostrich eyes with eager glint
a stone—his after-dinner mint.

It is a snack that he must swallow
so indigestion will not follow.

OALA

Koalas decorate the trees,
munching eucalyptus leaves.

This isn't *just* their favorite treat—
it is the *only* thing they eat.

PUFFIN

The puffin dives for little fish
with feats of derring-do,

Then takes its chick the tasty dish—
the chick likes herring, too.

NTEATER

With slender snout and sticky tongue equipped,
the anteater into an anthill dipped.

And while he dined was unaware, no doubt,
of little snacks escaping up his snout.

TICK BIRD

Tick birds ride the rhino's back,
looking for a tasty snack.

The rhino tolerates these guests
because they rid him of his pests.

RACCOON

Raccoons are not a fussy clan
when it comes time to eat.

They'll even raid a garbage can
to find a midnight treat.

FRUIT BAT

Fruit bats hanging by their feet
select some juicy grapes to eat.

This puzzles me and makes me frown.
How do they do it upside down?

SEA OTTER

The sea otter really prefers to recline

on his waterproof back in the kelp and the brine.

Abalone and clams are his favorite snacks.

He hammers each shell with a stone 'til it cracks.

FISH

The sea is full of fish.

For food they do not lack.

But here I can't distinguish

the snacker from the snack!

Would You Like to Make Your Own Animal Snackers?

I'll give you three ingredients
to make your own creation.

The fourth ingredient must be
your own imagination.

RECIPE

1 cup all purpose flour
½ **cup water**
½ **cup table salt**

In a bowl, mix all ingredients thoroughly.
Turn dough out onto a bread board, or any smooth surface.
Knead until dough is smooth and elastic and does not
stick to your hands.
Working as you would with clay, create your animal snackers
on an ungreased cookie sheet. Bake in a 325 degree oven
for ½ hour, or until dough feels firm to the touch.

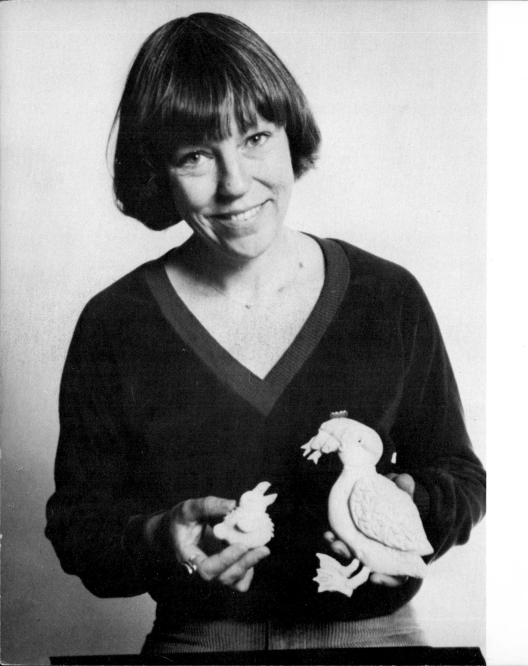

BETSY REILLY LEWIN grew up
in Clearfield, Pennsylvania.
She is a graduate of Pratt
Institute of Art in Brooklyn,
New York, where she met her
husband, Ted, also an author
and illustrator.

The Lewins now make their
home in Brooklyn in a
hundred-year-old brownstone.
Mrs. Lewin has designed
greeting cards and written
and illustrated stories for
a children's magazine.
This is her first book.